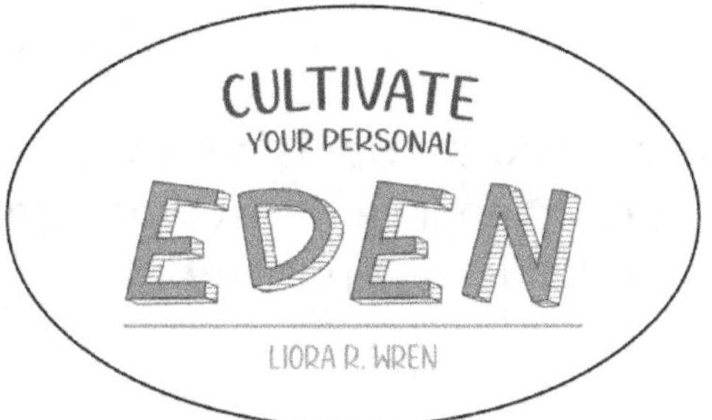

CULTIVATE
YOUR PERSONAL
EDEN
LIORA R. WREN

"Every small container is a lesson in beginning, a reminder that what grows is largely up to us." – Anonymous

In the bustling rhythms of modern life, where concrete often overshadows greenery, container gardening emerges as a beacon of hope for those yearning to reconnect with nature. This book, "Cultivate Your Personal Eden," is not merely a guide but an invitation to discover the joys and profound satisfactions of container gardening.

The beauty of container gardening lies in its simplicity and accessibility. You don't need vast tracts of land or years of gardening experience to start. A small balcony, patio, or even a windowsill suffices to embark on this green journey. Container gardening is about making the most of what you have, turning limited spaces into lush, thriving gardens that can feed the soul as much as they can fill your plates with home-grown produce.

Beyond the aesthetic appeal, container gardening offers practical benefits. It provides a sense of accomplishment and serenity, a break from the digital world, and a step towards sustainability by growing your own food. It's about creating life and nurturing it, learning lessons of patience, care, and resilience that plants teach us so well.

As you flip through these pages, you'll find not just instructions, but stories of growth, renewal, and connection. Whether you're a seasoned gardener looking to adapt to a smaller space or a complete novice with a desire to grow your first plant, this book is for you. It's designed to guide you through every step of your container gardening journey, from choosing your containers and plants to troubleshooting common issues.

So, I invite you to join me in this rewarding venture of container gardening. May you find in it the same joy, peace, and fulfillment that countless others have discovered—a personal Eden, where you can cultivate not just plants, but a deeper connection with life itself.

INDEX

Introduction

Container gardening is an enchanting journey that turns small spaces into areas of beauty and productivity. Whether you have a sprawling backyard or a modest balcony, the magic of container gardening allows you to cultivate a wide variety of plants, from lush flowers to fresh vegetables and herbs. This chapter lays the foundation for beginners, highlighting the benefits and the immense possibilities that container gardening brings.

The Essence of Container Gardening:
At its core, container gardening is about growing plants in pots or containers instead of planting them in the ground. This method offers flexibility, control over soil conditions, and an artistic element of design in gardening. It's an ideal solution for gardening enthusiasts living in urban areas or those with limited mobility, allowing them to create a garden oasis on patios, balconies, or even windowsills.

Why Choose Container Gardening?

- **Space Efficiency:** No matter how small your living space, there's always room for a pot or two. Container gardening makes it possible to green even the tiniest of spaces.
- **Versatility:** Containers can be moved to optimize plant health and aesthetic appeal. This mobility is perfect for adjusting to changing light conditions and temperatures.
- **Control:** You have complete control over the soil, water, and nutrients your plants receive. This is particularly beneficial for growing plants that have specific soil needs.
- **Accessibility:** Gardening in containers brings the garden to a comfortable height, which is a boon for individuals with physical constraints.
- **Aesthetic Appeal:** Containers add visual interest and a touch of personality to your gardening space. They can be as expressive and creative as you like.

What Can You Grow?

Almost anything that grows in a traditional garden can be adapted to container life. From annuals and perennials to vegetables, herbs, and even small trees and shrubs, your options are vast. The key is understanding the needs of each plant and choosing the right container to accommodate those needs.

As you embark on your container gardening journey, remember that each plant you nurture is a reflection of your care and dedication. Container gardening is not just about beautifying spaces or growing food; it's about cultivating joy and a sense of accomplishment from watching your garden thrive. In the coming chapters, we'll guide you through the essentials—selecting containers, preparing soil, choosing plants, and caring for your garden—turning your space into a personal Eden, no matter its size.

Chapter 1: Planning Your Container Garden

The foundation of a successful container garden lies in thoughtful planning. Before you embark on your gardening journey, it's crucial to lay the groundwork with careful consideration of your space and its unique characteristics. This chapter is designed to guide you through the initial planning phase, setting you up for success from the very beginning.

Assessing Your Space and Light Availability

Understanding Your Space:
Evaluating the space you have is the first step toward a flourishing container garden. It's not just about how much room you have but also how you envision using it. Consider the practical aspects, such as ease of access for regular maintenance and water supply. Also, think about the visibility of your garden; after all, part of its charm lies in its ability to transform your living space

aesthetically. Whether you're working with an expansive balcony, a cozy patio, or just a sunny windowsill, recognize that each setting has its own potential and limitations. It's about making the most of what you have and turning any area into a productive and beautiful green retreat.

Lighting Conditions:

Plants are as responsive to light as we are to a hearty meal—it's essential for their survival and vitality. Begin by observing the patterns of sunlight that grace your potential gardening space. Does the area bask in full sun for the majority of the day, or is it graced with a gentler patch of partial sun? Perhaps it's an area that's predominantly shaded. Understanding these conditions is not about limiting your choices but about finding plants that will thrive in the environment you can provide. This knowledge empowers you to make informed decisions, selecting plants that will flourish under your care.

Choosing Containers: Materials, Sizes, and Styles

Container Materials:
The materials from which your containers are made can have a significant impact on both the well-being of your plants and the overall aesthetic of your garden. Each material—from the lightweight flexibility of plastic to the breathable quality of terra cotta—carries with it a set of characteristics that can either complement or complicate your gardening efforts. Plastic pots are durable and come in a myriad of shapes and colors, but they may not offer the same breathability as natural terra cotta. Metal and wood, while stylish, can require additional considerations for durability and weight. Your choice should balance practicality with the visual appeal that

matches your personal style and the theme of your space.

Sizes and Styles:
Size matters when it comes to container gardening. A pot that's too small can restrict root growth and limit the potential of a plant, while an overly large one can lead to waterlogged soil and root rot. It's about finding the Goldilocks zone for your green companions—the perfect size for healthy growth. As for style, containers are your canvases; they are an expression of your taste and creativity. They can range from minimalist modern designs that suit a sleek urban balcony to rustic clay pots that evoke the charm of a country garden. Choose

containers that not only support the health of your plants but also reflect your vision of a personal Eden.

Planning your container garden by assessing your space and choosing the right containers sets the stage for gardening success. By understanding your environment and selecting containers that fit your aesthetic and practical needs, you're one step closer to creating your own personal Eden.

By giving attention to the foundational aspects of space, light, and container selection, you're paving the way for a container garden that's not just a haphazard array of plants but a thoughtfully curated extension of your living space. This is your first step towards cultivating your personal Eden—an oasis of green that offers both solace and joy.

Chapter 2: Selecting Your Plants

Choosing the right plants for your container garden is both an art and a science. It's about understanding the needs and compatibility of different species while also unleashing your creativity for beautiful compositions. This chapter will guide you through selecting the best plants for container gardening, taking into account their size, growth habits, and care requirements. Furthermore, we'll explore the aesthetic side of plant selection, teaching you how to mix and match for the most visually pleasing arrangements.

Best Plants for Container Gardening

Vegetables and Herbs:
One of the most rewarding aspects of container gardening is the ability to grow your own food. Vegetables and herbs are not only practical and delicious additions to your garden; they can also be quite ornamental. Plants like cherry tomatoes, bell peppers, leafy greens, and aromatic herbs such as basil, mint, and cilantro are perfect for containers. They not only bring freshness to your table but also greenery to your space. When choosing containers for edibles, consider the root depth and the mature size of the plants to ensure they have ample room to flourish.

Flowers and Ornamentals:

Flowering plants and ornamentals are the jewels of the garden, offering a burst of color, intriguing textures, and enchanting fragrances. Choices like petunias, marigolds, and geraniums are excellent for their long-lasting blooms and ease of care. Succulents, with their array of forms and minimal water requirements, offer a modern touch and are particularly suited for busy gardeners. Each plant adds its own unique aesthetic, and when chosen thoughtfully, can create a tapestry of color and interest in your container garden.

Mixing and Matching Plants for Visual Appeal

Creating Combinations:
The key to a stunning container garden is in the combination of plants you choose. By playing with height, using 'thrillers' for drama, 'fillers' to flesh out the body, and 'spillers' to cascade over the edges, you create layers of interest. It's important to consider not just the visual impact but also the growing conditions; plants with similar light and water needs will thrive together and make maintenance easier.

Theme Gardens:
Themed gardens can bring a sense of cohesion and narrative to your container gardening. Whether it's a vibrant salad garden with all the ingredients for a summer salad, a pollinator-friendly collection attracting bees and butterflies, or a Mediterranean-inspired assortment of herbs, a theme can guide your plant selection and provide creative direction.

Selecting plants for your container garden is more than just filling pots with soil and seeds; it's a process of envisioning and creating your own living art. The plants you choose and the way

you combine them will define the character of your garden. So, get creative, have fun, and watch as your space transforms into an abundant, bloom-filled sanctuary.

Chapter 3: The Right Soil and Compost

The essence of a vibrant container garden lies in the quality of the soil. This chapter addresses the pivotal role soil plays in container gardening and provides you with the knowledge to create the most nurturing environment for your plants. From selecting the right soil mix to creating your own, you will learn how to lay the perfect foundation for your garden to prosper.

Importance of Quality Soil

Why Soil Quality Matters:

The soil in your containers is the primary source of nutrients for your plants. Quality soil acts as a reservoir, supplying roots with water, nutrients, and oxygen—three critical ingredients for plant health. Unlike the in-ground soil that might contain pathogens or pests, a high-quality potting mix is designed to be disease-free, ensuring a safer environment for your plants to grow. We'll explore the distinct differences between garden soil and potting mix, highlighting why the latter is specifically tailored for the unique conditions of container gardening.

Benefits of Good Potting Mix:
A well-crafted potting mix is not just soil—it's a blend of components that work together to support your plants. It provides superior drainage, preventing water from pooling at the roots, which can cause rot. It also ensures proper aeration, allowing roots to breathe and preventing compaction often found in garden soils. The inclusion of organic matter within the mix acts as a slow-releasing fertilizer, nourishing your plants over time. We will delve into how these

elements work synergistically to foster robust growth and enhance the overall health of your garden.

Creating the Perfect Mix for Containers Components of a Good Potting Mix:

To create a conducive growing environment, you need the right mix of ingredients. Peat moss or coconut coir are excellent for moisture retention, giving your plants a consistent supply of water. Vermiculite or perlite adds to the mix's porosity, ensuring good airflow to the roots and preventing soil compaction. Compost is the heart of the mix, enriching it with a wealth of nutrients and beneficial microorganisms. Each of these components plays a crucial role in supporting a healthy container ecosystem.

DIY Potting Mix Recipes:
Equipped with the knowledge of what makes a good potting mix, you'll be ready to create your own. This section offers easy-to-follow recipes for crafting the ideal soil blend for your container garden. Whether your plants are drought-tolerant or water-loving, you'll learn how to adjust the components to suit their needs. From succulents to leafy greens, you'll have the instructions to mix the perfect home for each type of plant.

Adding Compost to Your Mix:
Incorporating compost into your potting mix can transform a good soil mix into a great one. Compost provides a dense nutrient profile and introduces beneficial microbes that can help in disease resistance and nutrient absorption. This section discusses the value of compost and guides you on how to mix it into your potting soil effectively, ensuring that your plants get the best possible start.

In crafting the right soil mix for your container garden, you are not just filling a vessel—you are creating a life-supporting habitat for your plants. This delicate balance of moisture, aeration, and nutrition is critical for plant health and vigor. Here, we provide the knowledge and techniques necessary to cultivate a soil environment that will act as the foundation for a thriving garden.

Understanding and creating the right soil mix for your container garden is foundational to your plants' success. The right balance of aeration, moisture retention, and nutrients will not only encourage vigorous growth but also bolster the resilience of your plants against pests and diseases. Remember, the health of your soil is directly proportional to the health of your plants. In the pages that follow, we'll ensure you have all the tools and information you need to create the most nurturing environment for your container garden. With healthy soil, you set the stage for your plants to thrive, bloom, and produce to their fullest potential.
The rich, fertile earth that you'll learn to create is not just soil; it's the cradle of life for your garden. Each scoop holds the

promise of growth, the scent of flowers, the taste of fresh vegetables, and the sheer joy of gardening. So let's get our hands dirty and our hearts full as we cultivate not just plants, but a deeper connection with the natural world through our container gardens.

Chapter 4: Planting Your Containers

Planting your containers is akin to painting a landscape where the soil is your canvas, and the plants are your palette of colors. This exhilarating process is a blend of science, art, and personal expression. This chapter will be your guide to translating the vision of your container garden into a living reality, ensuring each plant is given the best start in its new home.

Step-by-Step Planting Guide

1. Choosing Your Container:

Your choice of container is the first crucial step in the planting process. The size should accommodate the plant's growth, and the material should complement your garden's aesthetic. But beyond looks, functionality is key—adequate drainage is a must to prevent waterlogged soil which can lead to root rot.

2. Preparing Your Potting Mix:

Quality soil is the cornerstone of plant health. Refer to Chapter 3 for guidance on creating or choosing the right potting mix for your needs. Fill the container with this mix, leaving about an inch of space at the top to facilitate watering and prevent overflow.

3. Arranging Your Plants:

Position your plants while they're still in their nursery pots, experimenting with different arrangements. This pre-planting layout allows you to play with design elements such as color, height, and texture before making any commitments.

4. Planting:

With the layout set, it's time to transplant. Ease your plants out of their nursery pots, taking care not to damage the roots. If they are root-bound, gently tease the roots apart. Plant them at the same depth they were in their original containers, and backfill with your potting mix. Gently firm the soil to remove air pockets.

5. Watering:

Once all your plants are in place, give them a thorough watering. This initial watering is critical to help settle the soil around the roots and eliminate any air gaps. Water slowly and deeply, ensuring that moisture reaches the bottom of the container. This will also test the drainage of your container—water should flow freely out of the drainage holes, indicating that your soil mix and container are well-prepared to support plant health.

Tips for Arrangement and Aesthetics

Creating Visual Interest:
A beautifully planted container is more than just a collection of plants; it's a composition that captures the eye and evokes emotion. To achieve this, incorporate plants of varying heights, textures, and colors. Utilize the "thriller, filler, spiller" concept as a guideline for creating dynamic and visually interesting

container gardens. "Thrillers" add height and drama, "fillers" cover the soil and add body, while "spillers" cascade over the edges, softening the container's appearance.

Consider the View:

Your container's location plays a significant role in its arrangement. For containers that will be viewed from all angles, center your tallest plants and surround them with lower-growing fillers and spillers. If the container will be viewed from one side, place taller plants at the back and graduate down to shorter ones at the front. This creates depth and ensures every plant is visible.

Play with Color:

Color can dramatically affect the mood of your garden. Warm colors (reds, oranges, yellows) create a sense of excitement and vibrancy, while cool colors (blues, purples, greens) evoke calmness and tranquility. Don't shy away from experimenting with color combinations to find what pleases you. Whether you prefer bold contrasts, subtle gradations, or a monochromatic scheme, color is a powerful tool in your gardening arsenal.

Planting your containers is the moment your garden begins to take shape. With careful attention to the needs of your plants and a creative approach to their arrangement, you can create not just a garden, but a living work of art. As you progress, remember to trust your instincts and let your creativity flourish. Gardening is not just about the end result but the joy and fulfillment found in the process. Let your container gardens be a reflection of your unique vision and passion for the natural world.

Chapter 5: Watering and Feeding Your Garden

Ensuring the health and productivity of your container garden hinges on mastering the arts of watering and feeding. This chapter delves into the nuances of providing your plants with the hydration and nutrients they need to thrive. Adopting the right techniques for watering and fertilizing can significantly impact your garden's vitality, transforming it into a lush, flourishing oasis.

Watering Techniques for Healthy Plants

Understanding Your Plants' Water Needs:

Water is as vital to plants as air is to us, yet too much or too little can spell disaster. Different species of plants have unique requirements for water, influenced by their native habitats, growth stages, and the current weather conditions. Recognizing these needs is crucial. Always check the soil's moisture level—a simple finger test can tell you if it's time to water. This attentiveness ensures that each plant receives just the right amount of water to thrive.

How to Water:

Watering your plants correctly is about more than just frequency; it's about method. Aim to water deeply, saturating the soil to reach the roots where it's most needed, rather than a superficial sprinkle. This encourages plants to develop deeper root systems, enhancing their stability and access to nutrients. Morning or late afternoon watering reduces water loss through evaporation, ensuring that your plants get the full benefit of each watering session.

Tools and Tips for Efficient Watering:

Various tools can make watering both easier and more effective. Watering cans with long spouts, for instance, allow you to target the water directly to the soil, minimizing waste. Drip irrigation systems and self-watering containers offer more automated solutions, delivering water directly to the root zone where it's most needed. Additionally, mulching your containers can help retain soil moisture, reducing the need for frequent waterings and protecting against temperature extremes.

Fertilizing: What You Need to Know

The Role of Fertilizers:
Fertilizers play a crucial role in container gardening by replenishing the nutrients that plants exhaust from their growing medium. Regular watering can cause these nutrients to leach out of the soil, necessitating their replacement to maintain plant health. Fertilizers ensure that your plants have access to the essential minerals they need for growth, flowering, and fruiting.

Types of Fertilizers:

The world of fertilizers is vast, with options ranging from slow-release granules to liquid feeds, organic composts to synthetic mixes. Each type has its benefits, from the immediacy of liquid fertilizers to the sustained release of granules. Organic options, such as compost or fish emulsion, also improve soil structure and microbial health. Selecting the right fertilizer depends on your gardening goals and the specific needs of your plants.

How and When to Fertilize:

Frequency and timing are key in fertilization. Over-fertilizing can harm your plants as much as under-fertilizing.

Generally, a regular feeding schedule tailored to the growth phase of your plants—more frequent for fast-growing vegetables and flowers, less so for slower-growing shrubs and perennials—will yield the best results. Always follow the instructions on the fertilizer packaging to avoid nutrient burn.

Signs of Over- or Under-Fertilization:
Learning to read your plants is essential. Symptoms like yellowing leaves, stunted growth, or leaf burn can indicate nutrient imbalances. If you suspect an issue, assess your fertilization routine and adjust accordingly. Sometimes, flushing the soil with water to remove excess nutrients can help rebalance the soil's chemistry.

By mastering the essentials of watering and feeding, you equip yourself with the tools to nurture a container garden that's both vibrant and productive. It's a delicate balance, but with attentiveness and care, you can create a garden that's as bountiful as it is beautiful. Remember, the secret to a thriving garden lies in

understanding and catering to the needs of your plants, allowing your green space to reach its full potential.

Chapter 6: Maximizing Light and Location

Light plays a pivotal role in the life of a plant, influencing its growth, bloom, and overall health. In the dynamic world of container gardening, you have the unique

opportunity to optimize light exposure to meet the specific needs of your plants. This chapter sheds light on the importance of sunlight in gardening and provides practical advice for harnessing its power to enhance the growth of your container plants.

Understanding Sun Requirements

The Spectrum of Sunlight Needs:
Plants have evolved to thrive under specific light conditions, categorized

broadly as full sun, partial sun/shade, and full shade. Each category has distinct characteristics that influence plant health and productivity. Full sun plants flourish under direct sunlight for most of the day, partial sun/shade plants require a delicate balance of light and shade, while full shade plants thrive in minimal direct sunlight. Recognizing these needs is essential for plant selection, ensuring your garden is composed of species that will thrive in the light conditions you can provide.

Assessing Your Available Light:
Before selecting your plants, it's important to assess the light conditions of your intended gardening space. Monitoring how sunlight moves across the area at different times of the day and throughout the seasons will give you a clear understanding of what you're working with. Utilize tools like sun calculators or apps to measure light intensity in specific spots, helping you match your plant choices to the available light.

Positioning Containers for Optimal Growth

Strategic Placement:
The beauty of container gardening lies in its versatility. If certain areas of your space receive more light than others, you can strategically place your containers to ensure each plant receives its ideal amount of sunlight. Consider the mobility of containers as an advantage—rotating and rearranging them not only prevents uneven growth and leaning but also allows you to adapt to the changing light conditions throughout the day and seasons.

Adjusting to Seasons:
The sun's path shifts with the seasons, affecting the intensity and duration of sunlight your garden receives. Understanding these changes is crucial for maintaining optimal growth conditions year-round. Adjust the placement of your containers as needed to capitalize on the available sunlight, moving plants to catch the summer sun or to protect them from the harsher rays.

Utilizing Reflective Surfaces:
In areas where natural light is limited, reflective surfaces can be a gardener's best friend. By strategically placing mirrors or painting walls with light-reflecting colors, you can amplify the available light, ensuring even the shadier spots of your garden benefit from enhanced illumination. This technique can be particularly effective in urban settings, where buildings may block direct sunlight for parts of the day.

Maximizing the light and optimizing the location of your container garden significantly contributes to the vitality of your plants. By understanding the specific light needs of your garden's inhabitants and employing strategies to meet these needs, you create an environment where your plants can not only survive but thrive. Container gardening's inherent flexibility offers endless possibilities for experimentation and adjustment, empowering you to cultivate a lush, healthy garden in any space.

Chapter 7: Ongoing Care and Maintenance

Introduction:
The joy of container gardening continues well beyond the initial planting. Ongoing care and maintenance are key to sustaining vibrant, healthy plants. This chapter covers the essentials of pruning, deadheading, repotting, and pest and disease management—ensuring your garden remains a source of beauty and fulfillment.

Pruning, Deadheading, and Repotting

Pruning for Health and Shape:
Explain the importance of pruning to remove dead or overgrown branches, which helps encourage healthy growth and maintain the plant's shape. Offer step-by-step instructions on how to prune effectively.

The Benefits of Deadheading:

Detail the process of deadheading—removing spent flowers—to promote more blooms and extend the flowering period. Clarify which types of plants benefit most from this practice.

Knowing When to Repot:

Provide guidance on recognizing signs that a plant needs repotting, such as roots growing through drainage holes or slowed growth. Include a brief tutorial on how to repot a plant safely.

Monitoring and Managing Pests and Diseases

Identifying Common Pests:
Introduce the most common pests in container gardening, such as aphids, spider mites, and whiteflies. Offer visual

aids to help identify these pests and early signs of infestation.

Natural and Chemical Control Methods: Discuss both natural remedies and safe chemical treatments for managing pests. Emphasize the importance of early detection and intervention.

Disease Prevention and Management:

Outline strategies for preventing plant diseases, such as ensuring proper air circulation and avoiding overwatering. Provide advice on treating common diseases should they arise.

Regular care and maintenance are the keys to a thriving container garden. By staying vigilant and responding to the needs of your plants—through pruning, deadheading, repotting, and pest and disease management—you can enjoy a lush, vibrant garden throughout the year. Remember, a little effort goes a long way in keeping your garden healthy and flourishing.

Chapter 8: Seasonal Considerations

A container garden is an ever-changing tapestry that reflects the rhythm of the seasons. Each season brings its own set of tasks, challenges, and joys. Understanding how to adapt your gardening practices to the seasonal shifts is crucial for a garden that thrives year-round. This chapter guides you through the essential considerations and adjustments needed to harmonize your gardening efforts with the natural cycle of the seasons.

Adapting Your Container Garden to the Seasons

Spring: A Time for Planting and Renewal: Spring heralds a new beginning, an opportunity to refresh your garden. Updating potting soil, selecting seasonal plants, and starting seedlings are all crucial steps in awakening your garden from its winter slumber. This is the time to plan and plant with anticipation for the months ahead.

Summer: Maintaining Vigor and Bloom:
The abundance of summer demands diligent care. Regular watering, consistent fertilization, and ongoing pest management are key to sustaining your garden's vibrancy. Monitoring plants for signs of heat stress and providing shade when necessary can prevent scorching and ensure continued growth.

Autumn: Preparation and Transition:

As the days shorten, your garden requires preparation for the cooler months. Pruning, applying mulch, and considering which plants to bring indoors are all pivotal steps. Autumn is also a time to plant cool-season crops and savor the beauty of fall-blooming species.

Winter Care and Indoor Options:

Protecting Plants from Cold:
Winter poses a significant challenge, particularly for outdoor container plants. Strategies for frost protection, such as clustering containers for shared warmth, utilizing frost cloths, or relocating plants to a more sheltered spot, are vital for their survival.

Indoor Gardening Tips:
For plants that spend winter indoors, creating an environment that closely mimics their outdoor conditions is key. This involves managing light exposure, temperature, and humidity levels to prevent stress and encourage continued growth. Employing grow lights can compensate for shorter daylight hours, ensuring your plants receive sufficient light. Additionally, using humidifiers or placing water trays near heating sources can help maintain the humidity levels many plants crave during the dry winter months.

Seasonal changes bring a dynamic aspect to container gardening, presenting an opportunity to engage

with your garden in a way that aligns with the natural world. By understanding and anticipating these changes, you can adapt your care approach to support your garden's health and vibrancy throughout the year. Whether it's nurturing seedlings in the spring, ensuring hydration and protection in the summer, preparing for the cooler autumn months, or transitioning into indoor gardening for winter, each season offers unique challenges and rewards.

Embracing the seasonal rhythm allows you to not only maintain a garden that is resilient and thriving but also deepens your connection to the cycle of life and the environment around you. With each change of season, your container garden offers new lessons, joys, and the continued promise of growth and renewal.

Chapter 9: Harvesting and Enjoying Your Garden

Harvesting the fruits of your labor is perhaps the most gratifying aspect of container gardening. Beyond the tangible rewards of fresh, home-grown produce, the sensory and aesthetic pleasures of your garden contribute to a deeper sense of achievement and connection with nature. This chapter aims to guide you through harvesting your bounty and maximizing the enjoyment of your garden's beauty.

Tips for Harvesting Edibles

Knowing When to Harvest:

The timing of your harvest can significantly impact the quality and quantity of your yield. Each vegetable and herb has indicators for optimal harvest time, such as size, color, and firmness. For instance, tomatoes are best picked when they've reached their full color and have a slight give under gentle pressure. Herbs, on the other hand, are most potent when harvested in the morning after the dew has dried but before the sun is high. Timely harvesting not only ensures the best flavor but can also stimulate further production, extending your garden's bounty.

Harvesting Techniques:
Proper technique is crucial to harvesting your plants without causing damage to them or their future yield. Gentle handling is key. Use clean, sharp tools like scissors or pruning shears for precise cuts, reducing stress on the plant. For leafy greens, pick from the outer leaves to allow the center leaves to continue growing. This section will provide specific techniques tailored to different types of

edibles, ensuring you harvest your crops effectively and safely.

Storing Your Harvest:
Maximizing the freshness and longevity of your harvest is essential. Different types of produce require varying storage methods. Cool, dark places are ideal for root vegetables, while leafy greens thrive in the humidity of refrigerator crispers. Herbs can be kept fresh in water at room temperature or dried for long-term storage. This part of the chapter will offer practical advice on cleaning, drying, and storing your produce, helping you enjoy the fruits of your garden for as long as possible.

Enjoying the Beauty of Your Container Garden

Creating Outdoor Living Spaces:
Your container garden can transform any outdoor area into a vibrant living space. Arrange your plants to create natural privacy screens, shaded retreats, or colorful focal points. This section will inspire you to view your garden as an

extension of your home, offering design ideas that enhance both the functionality and aesthetics of your outdoor spaces.

Photographing Your Garden:
Documenting the growth and evolution of your garden can be a fulfilling endeavor. Photography not only allows you to capture the fleeting beauty of your plants but also to reflect on your gardening journey. Tips on lighting, composition, and perspective will help you take stunning photos that tell the story of your garden, preserving these moments for years to come.

Sharing with Community:
One of the greatest joys of gardening is sharing its bounty and beauty with others. Whether it's hosting a garden party, exchanging produce with neighbors, or donating to local food banks, your garden can be a source of connection and community. This section will explore the various ways you can share your garden's abundance, spreading the joy and fulfillment that comes from gardening.

The experience of harvesting and enjoying your container garden encompasses more than just the yield— it's about the pleasure of nurturing life, the delight in its beauty, and the warmth of sharing it with others. As you continue on your gardening path, take time to appreciate these moments, for they embody the essence of what it means to garden.

Chapter 10: Troubleshooting Common Issues

A flourishing container garden is the result of attentive care and proactive problem-solving. Despite your best efforts, you may encounter challenges such as pests, diseases, or environmental stressors. This chapter equips you with the knowledge to identify and resolve common issues, ensuring your garden's resilience and vitality.

Identifying and Solving Common Problems

Watering Issues: Overwatering and Underwatering.

Watering is a balancing act; too much or too little can adversely affect your plants. Overwatering leads to yellowing leaves and soggy soil, which can cause root rot, while underwatering results in dry soil and drooping leaves, stressing the plant. To avoid these issues, establish a consistent watering schedule tailored to each plant's needs and regularly check soil moisture. This section will guide you on how to adjust your watering practices to prevent over or underwatering effectively.

Pest Infestations:

Pests can quickly turn a thriving garden into a struggling one. Identifying an infestation early is crucial for effective management. Look for signs like holes in leaves, sticky residues, or the pests themselves. This chapter offers strategies for controlling common pests such as aphids, spider mites, and whiteflies using both organic methods, like introducing beneficial insects, and safe chemical treatments when necessary.

Disease Prevention:
Diseases can stealthily undermine the health of your container garden. Common symptoms include unusual leaf spots, moldy coatings, and weakened stems. This part of the chapter focuses on preventive measures such as ensuring good air circulation, practicing crop rotation, and maintaining cleanliness around your plants. We'll also cover effective treatments for diseases like fungal infections and root rot, emphasizing the importance of early detection and action.

Nutrient Deficiencies:
Just like humans, plants can suffer from nutrient deficiencies, manifesting as chlorosis (yellowing leaves) or stunted growth. Correcting these deficiencies involves adjusting your fertilization regimen or supplementing with specific nutrients. This section provides a guide to diagnosing and treating nutrient

deficiencies, ensuring your plants receive a balanced diet for optimal health.

Preventive Measures for a Healthy Garden

Regular Monitoring and Maintenance:
Vigilance is key to a healthy garden. Regular monitoring allows for early problem detection, making management much more straightforward. This includes inspecting plants for signs of distress, cleaning up dead leaves and debris to minimize disease and pest habitats, and ensuring your gardening tools are clean and well-maintained.

Soil Health and Quality:
The foundation of garden health lies in the quality of your soil. Using a high-quality potting mix, enriching it with compost, and refreshing it periodically helps prevent many common gardening issues. This section reiterates the importance of soil health, offering tips on maintaining a nutritious and well-structured growing medium for your plants.

Proper Plant Selection:
Choosing the right plants for your garden's specific conditions is a crucial preventive measure against stress and disease. This includes considering light, temperature, and humidity requirements. By selecting plants that are well-suited to your garden's environment, you can significantly reduce the risk of stress-related problems.

Addressing common issues in container gardening requires a combination of careful observation, timely intervention, and preventive practices. By staying informed and proactive, you can navigate these challenges and maintain a garden that is not only healthy and productive but also a source of joy and beauty. Remember, a little effort in troubleshooting and maintenance can go a long way in ensuring the success and longevity of your container garden.

Conclusion

As we draw the curtain on our journey through the enchanting world of container gardening, it's essential to reflect on the journey we've embarked upon together. From the initial planning stages to the ongoing care and troubleshooting of common issues, we've navigated the multifaceted aspects of creating and maintaining a thriving container garden. Each chapter was designed not only to impart practical knowledge and skills but also to inspire you to explore the limitless possibilities that container gardening offers.

Container gardening is more than just a hobby; it's a gateway to a deeper connection with nature, a way to enhance our living spaces, and a means to cultivate beauty and sustenance regardless of the size of our outdoor spaces. The versatility and accessibility of container gardening make it a rewarding endeavor for gardeners of all levels of experience—from the novice to the seasoned green thumb.

The journey doesn't end here. Gardening is a lifelong learning experience, where each season brings new challenges and opportunities for growth, both for our plants and for ourselves as gardeners. The garden is a teacher, offering lessons in patience, resilience, and the rewards of careful nurturing. Your container garden will evolve, reflecting the time, care, and love you invest in it.

Remember to celebrate the successes, no matter how small, and to view any setbacks not as failures but as opportunities to learn and improve. Share the bounty and beauty of your garden with others, for the joy of gardening is magnified when it is shared.

As you continue on your gardening journey, may your containers overflow with vibrant blooms, lush foliage, and bountiful harvests. May y

our outdoor spaces become sanctuaries of peace and beauty, where you can connect with the rhythms of nature and the creative pulse of life.

Thank you for allowing this book to be a part of your gardening journey. Here's to the many seasons of joy, discovery, and growth that lie ahead in your container garden. May you cultivate not just plants, but a greener, more vibrant world, one container at a time.

Happy gardening!

9 7 9 8 8 6 9 2 6 8 8 3 9